To K

—Br

Text by Patricia Hegarty
Text copyright © 2016 by Little Tiger Press
Cover art and interior illustrations copyright © 2016 by Britta Teckentrup

All rights reserved. Published in the United States by Doubleday, an imprin
Random House Children's Books, a division of Penguin Random House LLC
Originally published in the United Kingdom by Little Tiger Press in 2016.

Doubleday and the colophon are registered trademarks of Penguin Random

Visit us on the Web! randomhousekids.com

Educators and librarians, for a variety of teaching tools, visit us at RHTeach

Library of Congress Cataloging-in-Publication Data
is available upon request.

ISBN 978-1-5247-1526-7 (trade)

MANUFACTURED IN CHINA
10 9 8 7 6 5 4 3 2 1
First American Edition

LTK/1800/0416/0916

BEE

A Peek-Through Picture Book

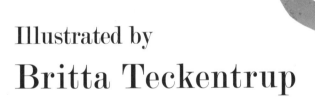

Illustrated by
Britta Teckentrup

DOUBLEDAY BOOKS FOR YOUNG READERS

Dawn is breaking on a brand-new day,
And in the meadow, poppies sway.

A bee appears, striped black and gold.
A wonder of nature is about to unfold.

In the treetops, birds start to sing.
The little bee beats her wings.

here and there,
ing fills the air.

Back and fort

Bee knows exac

Visiting flowers of every hue,
She has a special job to do.

Gathering nectar as she goes,
From every foxglove, every rose,
Dusty with pollen, the little bee
Buzzes, buzzes, busily.

Bee travels on from bloom to bloom,
Drawn in by their sweet perfume.

Harvesting flowers one by one,
Her compass is the midday sun.

Among the orchard's apple trees,
Blossoms quiver in the breeze.

Carrying pollen from place to place,
Bee always leaves a tiny trace.

Flowers as far as the eye can see.
Too many flowers for just one bee!

All of a sudden, Bee is gone.

She has a message to pass on.

Back at the hive, Bee spreads the news:
There's work to be done—no time to lose!

Listen for their gentle humming.
The word is out—the bees are coming!

Buzzing over the dense hedgerows,
Past the pond, where wild thyme grows . . .

Through the orchard's sweet-smelling scent,
The bees travel on with calm intent.

As lilies glow orange in the sun,
The bees must finish what they've begun . . .

Stopping at every flower they find,
Leaving the gift of pollen behind.

The bees pass over a woodland stream.

Droplets sparkle and pebbles gleam.

Water trickles, bubbles, and weaves.
A weeping willow trails its leaves.

As the bees fly on through buds and burs,
A tiny miracle occurs:

So many plants and flowers you see
Were given life by one small bee.